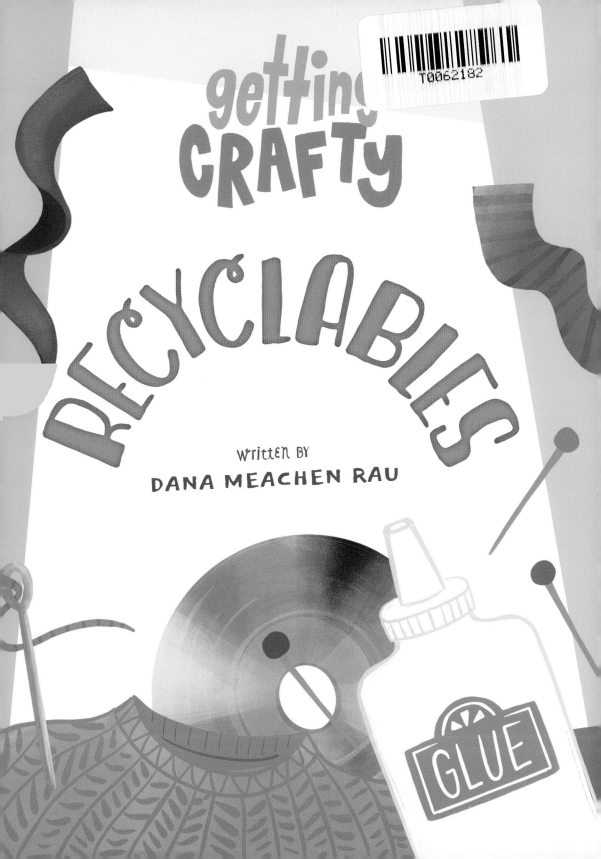

getting CRAFTY

RECYCLABLES

written by
DANA MEACHEN RAU

45TH PARALLEL PRESS

Published in the United States of America by Cherry Lake Publishing Group
Ann Arbor, Michigan
www.cherrylakepublishing.com

Reading Adviser: Beth Walker Gambro, MS, Ed., Reading Consultant, Yorkville, IL
Illustrator: Ashley Dugan
Book Designer: Felicia Macheske

Photo Credits: © Monkey Business Images/Shutterstock, 4; © InnaFelker/Shutterstock, 5; © UPPICHAYA/Shutterstock, 6; © Lee Yiu Tung, 7/Shutterstock; © Svetsol/Shutterstock, 7

45th Parallel Press is an imprint of Cherry Lake Publishing Group.

Library of Congress Cataloging-in-Publication Data

Names: Rau, Dana Meachen, 1971- author. | Dugan, Ashley, illustrator.
Title: Recyclables / written by Dana Meachen Rau ; illustrated by Ashley Dugan.
Description: Ann Arbor : Cherry Lake Publishing, [2023] | Series: Getting crafty | Includes bibliographical references and index. | Audience: Grades 4-6 | Summary: "Who says that's trash?! Explore your creative side and get crafty with items found in recycling bins! Discover new skills and learn how to create with recyclables such as paper, paint samples, old gift cards, and more! Book includes an introduction on the importance of recycling and upcycling. It also includes several projects with easy-to-follow step-by-step instructions and illustrations. Book is developed to aid struggling and reluctant readers with engaging content, carefully chosen vocabulary, and simple sentences. Includes table of contents, glossary, index, sidebars, and author biographies"—Provided by publisher.
Identifiers: LCCN 2022041811 | ISBN 9781668920596 (paperback) | ISBN 9781668919576 (hardcover) | ISBN 9781668923252 (pdf) | ISBN 9781668921920 (ebook)
Subjects: LCSH: Handicraft for children—Juvenile literature. | Salvage (Waste, etc.)—Juvenile literature. | Recycling (Waste, etc.)—Juvenile literature.
Classification: LCC TT160 .R3825 2023 | DDC 745.5083—dc23/eng/20220902
LC record available at https://lccn.loc.gov/2022041811

Cherry Lake Publishing Group would like to acknowledge the work of the Partnership for 21st Century Learning, a Network of Battelle for Kids. Please visit *http://www.battelleforkids.org/networks/p21* for more information.

Printed in the United States of America
Corporate Graphics

TABLE OF CONTENTS

ONE OF A KIND

What if everyone were the same? Life would be boring! How do you stand out from the crowd? What hobbies make you unique? What sports are you great at? Think about your interests, humor, or beliefs. All these things make you one of a kind!

You can make one-of-a-kind crafts too! They'll reflect your personality. Use recycled materials! That is a great way to make something unique.

Look around you at the items people throw in the trash. Banana peels are definitely garbage. But is the lid of a jar garbage? Or the ribbons from a gift? What about the pictures from an old calendar? These can all be made into something new. It will be a unique creation of your own!

TOO MUCH TRASH

What happens to trash? Most goes to a landfill. At a landfill trash is buried. It is covered with soil. We hope it will **decompose**. But some items can be reused. They don't need to go to the landfill.

Recycling means reusing an item again. Paper, glass, metal, and plastic can all be recycled. They can become new products. Paper can be shredded. It's mixed with water. Then it can become new kinds of paper. Metal, glass, and plastic can be melted. Then they are remolded into new forms.

Recycling helps our Earth. You can play a part in recycling too. Don't throw that jar away. Use it for a craft! This is called "upcycling."

THE RECYCLING SYMBOL

Recycling bins are marked with a picture of three arrows. They form a triangle. This is the symbol for recycling. It is used around the world. It is also on any item that can be recycled. It is on any item that is made from recycled materials.

ENDLESS SUPPLIES

Where can you find items to recycle into craft projects? Here are some ideas:

AROUND THE HOUSE

Check in the kitchen. You might find plastic lids, bottle caps, cardboard boxes, and more. Look in the closet. Look for clothing that is worn out or too small. Neckties, T-shirts, buttons, sweaters, or socks with holes can all be used. Magazines, newspapers, wrapping paper, nubs of crayons, or scraps of string can be reused, too. Be creative! Go on a recycling scavenger hunt.

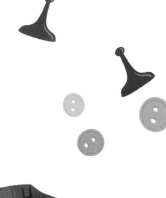

TAG SALES

People on your street might hold tag sales in their yard. These sales allow families to sell things they don't need anymore. Tag sales are great places to get furniture. You can find old board games and books. You can find other items. Things are at low prices.

FRIENDS AND FAMILY

Ask your friends or family! They might have items to share. Maybe you can offer to help them. Clean out a closet, basement, or attic with them. They might share treasures you find. You can use them for crafts.

BASIC TOOLS

Projects need different supplies. They need materials. Here is a list of some of the items you will need.

CUTTING TOOLS

Paper scissors work best for most projects. Fabric scissors are a little sharper. They cut through fabric and ribbon. A box cutter can cut into thick materials. Never use a box cutter without help from an adult. It is very sharp.

TAPE AND GLUE

Tape and glue are **adhesives**. There are many kinds. There is electrical tape. This is a **flexible** vinyl tape. It is safe for projects with wiring. There is varnish. Varnish is a glue. It hardens to a clear finish.

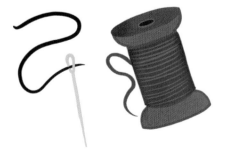

SEWING SUPPLIES

You will need a needle, thread, and straight pins. Use pins with large colorful heads. They are easier to hold. They are easier to find!

DRAWING SUPPLIES

Keep paper and pencils handy. Use it to make plans or patterns. Jot down ideas for new projects. Draw new ideas.

APPLIANCES AND TOOLS

Some of these projects need a blender, drill, light kit, and washing machine. Ask an adult for permission first. Ask for help. Never use them alone.

RECYCLABLE MATERIALS

The list of things to use is endless! You can use paper, metal, glass, and plastic. You can find a new use for almost anything! In this book, you will use the following:

- Scraps of ribbon, lace, and construction paper
- Paint samples
- An old piece of furniture
- An old wool sweater and T-shirt
- Old CDs or DVDs
- An old lamp shade
- An old book
- Used plastic gift cards

PAINTING and SEWING TIPS

PAINTING

There are two kinds of painting in this book. Acrylic paint adds pizzazz to projects. Decoupage (pronounced day-koo-PAHZH) is gluing paper to another surface. It's glued to glass or wood. You use varnish. Here are some tips:

- Keep things neat. Put newspapers over your work place. Wear an apron or smock.
- Use a paper plate as a **palette**. This holds paint or varnish.
- Clean your brush in warm, soapy water. Do this as soon as you're done! Use water-based paints and varnishes. They are easier to clean.
- You might need extra coats of paint or varnish.

SEWING

Sewing is a great way to attach fabric to a craft project.

Threading a needle: Make sure you have good light. Hold the needle steady. Poke the thread through the eye of the needle. It's tricky! Pull the thread through. Pull until the two ends meet. Tie them in a knot.

Running stitch: This is an in-and-out stitch. Poke the needle down into the fabric. Pull it until it stops at the knot. Poke the needle up through the fabric. Pull all the way through. Repeat until you reach the end. Keep your stitches straight. Keep them even.

Securing the end: How to finish stitching? Poke the needle in and out again. Do this very close together. Don't pull it all the way through yet. Poke the needle through the loop made by the thread. Then pull it all the way through. Repeat to make a double knot. Trim off the extra thread. Use fabric scissors.

FLASHY FLOWER SUN CATCHER

Do your parents have old CDs or DVDs? CDs played music. DVDs showed movies. Hang them in a window! The sparkly sides catch the sun. It makes rainbows!

MATERIALS

- Old CDs or DVDs
- Fine-tip and broad-tip permanent black markers
- Acrylic paint in a few colors
- Paintbrushes
- Invisible thread
- Scissors

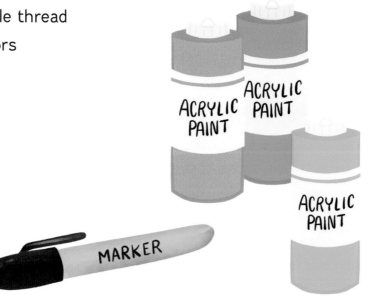

ACRYLIC PAINT

ACRYLIC PAINT

ACRYLIC PAINT

MARKER

STEPS

1. Doodle shapes or draw a pattern. Do this on the shiny surface of the disc. Use the markers. Be creative! There are no rules for creating your pattern.

2. Flip the disc over. Paint the other side with acrylic paint. Use a bright color. Let it dry.

3. Cut a long piece of invisible thread. Thread it through the center of the disc. Loop it around. Tie a knot at the edge of the disc. Tie a loop at the end of the thread.

4. Hang your sun catcher in a sunny window!

MAKING A MOBILE

Try using a few suncatchers to make a mobile. Tie the threads of three or more sun catchers side by side on a stick or rod. Then use invisible thread to hang up the rod.

T-SHIRT MAKEOVER

Make an old t-shirt into a fashion statement. Use beads or scraps of ribbon or lace. (Check with someone you know who sews!)

MATERIALS

- An old T-shirt
- Scraps of ribbon and lace
- Plastic beads
- Fabric scissors
- Pins
- Needle and thread
- Fabric markers (optional)

STEPS

1. Lay the T-shirt flat on your work surface. Cut off the **hems** of the sleeves. Cut off the hem of the shirt bottom. Cut each arm hem into one strip. Cut the bottom hem into two strips.

2. Sew a running stitch. Sew it along the edge of one of the strips. At the end, pull the thread. The fabric will scrunch up. Roll it up. It will look like a rose. Sew the bottom of the rose closed. Tie it with a knot.

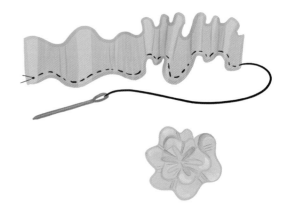

3. Repeat this step. Use the other strips. You'll have four roses.

4. Sew on a piece of ribbon or lace. Sew it around the neckline. Sew on the fabric roses, too.

5. Pin a wider ribbon or piece of lace on the back of the shirt. Pin it a few inches below the armholes. Sew it to the shirt. Use a running stitch on the top and bottom edge. You will tie this ribbon in the front when you wear it.

6. Fold each sleeve in half. Cut small triangles along the folded edge. Unfold the sleeve. You have a diamond pattern!

7. Cut strips along the bottom of the shirt. Cut even. Make fringe! Decorate the fringe with beads. Knot the end of each strip. You can also draw on your shirt. Use with fabric markers. It's all up to you!

front

back

SCRAP PAPER BOWL

Are you crafty? You probably have lots of paper scraps. They're left over from other projects. Don't throw them away! Make them into a colorful bowl. Construction paper is good for this project. It breaks down easily. But newspaper scraps work, too!

MATERIALS

- Scraps of construction paper
- Scissors
- Measuring cup
- Blender
- Water
- Spoon
- Strainer
- Paper towels
- A small bowl that fits snugly inside the strainer
- Dry sponge

STEPS

1. Cut the scraps of construction paper. Cut them into 1-inch (2.5 centimeter) squares. You need about a cup of them. Place them in the blender. Add 1 cup (237 milliliters) of water to the blender. Blend the water and paper together. It will become a mushy **pulp**.

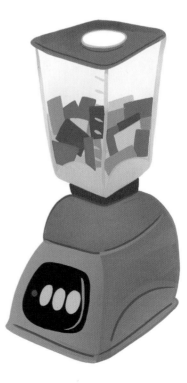

2. Work over the sink. Spoon the pulp into the strainer. Use the back of a spoon to push the water through the strainer. As you push the water out, spread the pulp around the strainer. Make it even all around.

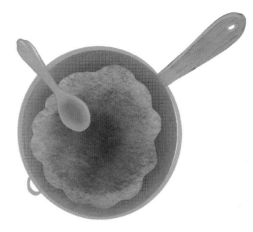

3. Place paper towels down on the counter. Place a small bowl upside down on top of them. Wrap the bowl in another piece of paper towel.

4. Flip the strainer upside down. Flip it onto the bowl. Use a dry sponge. Press all over the bottom of the strainer. Let the sponge soak up as much water as you can.

5. Lift the strainer from the pulp. Be careful. Let the paper bowl sit. Let it dry for 24 hours.

A UNIQUE LOOK
Try adding glitter, pine needles, or dryer lint when you blend your paper pulp together. This will give your project a unique look.

PAINT SAMPLE STOOL

Do you have an old stool around your house? Maybe it needs a colorful pick-me-up! Cut up old paint samples. Decoupage them onto the stool. Soon you'll be sitting pretty!

MATERIALS

- An old stool or other small piece of furniture
- Sandpaper
- Paint and paintbrush (optional)
- Colorful paint samples
- Scissors
- Sponge brush
- Water-based varnish
- Paper plate palette

STEPS

1. Sand the stool. Use sandpaper. This will smooth the surface. It will remove old paint or varnish. Does it still have a lot of old paint? You can repaint the stool. Use white or any color you want. Let it dry completely. Move to step **2**.

2. Cut the paint samples into small shapes. Pour some varnish onto your paper plate palette. Use a sponge brush. Paint some varnish on the top of the stool. Place a color shape on top. Then paint over the shape with varnish.

3. Repeat with more squares. Do this all over the top of the stool. You can overlap them. Cover the surface. Paint over the top of the stool with a coat of varnish.

4. Repeat steps **2** and **3** on the legs of your stool.

5. Let the stool dry until it is dry to the touch. It might take 2 hours. Add a second coat of varnish. Cover all over the top and legs. Let the stool dry. Wait at least 24 hours. Now you can use it!

THICK AND THIN

Paint samples are made on thick paper. They work best on flat surfaces. If your stool has rounded legs, use thinner paper. Try office paper, wrapping paper, or tissue paper.

EASY-TO-MAKE MITTENS

Have you washed a wool sweater in a washing machine? It shrinks! This is bad for your favorite sweater. But good for this project! Shrink an old sweater. Then use the new fabric to make mittens!

MATERIALS

- Old wool sweater (must be 100 percent wool, not washable wool)
- Washing machine, laundry soap, and towel
- Pencil, paper, and scissors
- Fabric scissors
- Pins
- Needle and thread

STEPS

1. Put the sweater in a washing machine. Add a little bit of laundry soap. Wash it at the hottest setting. It will shrink into a tight fabric. Can you still see separate stitches? Wash it again. Lay it on a towel. Let it dry.

2. Trace a mitten shape. Trace around your hand on a piece of paper. Draw the line about 0.5 inch (1.3 cm) larger than your hand. Cut out the shape. Use scissors. This is your pattern.

3. Pin your pattern onto the sweater fabric. Use fabric scissors. Cut out the fabric. Repeat three more times. You will have four mitten shapes.

4. Match up two of the shapes. Use a needle and thread. Sew from the wrist, around the thumb, around the top, and back to the other wrist end. Tie the thread with a knot. Leave the bottom of the mitten open.

5. Turn the mitten right side out.

6. Repeat steps 4 and 5. Use the other two mitten shapes.

GIFT CARD CHANDELIER

Gift cards are good gifts. But they get thrown away after they're used. Collect your old cards. Ask friends and family to do the same. Visit tag sales. Find an old lampshade. Purchase a hanging light kit. Most hardware stores have them. It's a socket on the end of an electrical cord.

MATERIALS

- Old lamp shade with **diameter** of 10 to 12 inches (25 to 30 cm)
- Hanging light kit (use a bulb marked "CfL" or "LeD")
- Black electrical tape
- About 45 gift cards
- Electric hand drill with 0.125-inch (3 millimeter) bit
- Thin black ribbon
- Scissors

STEPS

1. Remove all of the fabric from the lampshade. You'll be left with just the top metal frame. Attach the hanging light kit to the lampshade frame. Ask an adult to help.

2. Wind electrical tape around the metal frame of the lampshade.

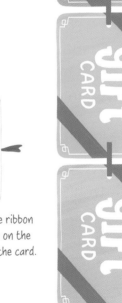

3. Ask an adult to drill holes in each gift card. There should be a hole at the top and bottom. Make the hole about 0.25 inch (0.6 cm) from the edge. Plan how you will arrange your cards. You will need three rows of cards.

4. Cut the ribbon into 12-inch (30 cm) pieces. Thread the ribbon in and out through the holes. Don't weave out through the last hole.

5. Tape the ribbon to the back of each card. Use electrical tape. Trim the bottom end of the ribbon. Leave a tail at the top.

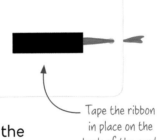

Tape the ribbon in place on the back of the card.

6. Loop the top tail of ribbon over the rim of the lampshade. Tape the ribbon to the back of the top card. Trim the extra ribbon. Repeat with the rest of the cards and ribbon.

HOW TO HANG YOUR CHANDELIER

Hang your new light from the ceiling. You will need two hooks. Have an adult screw them into the ceiling. One goes above the outlet where you will plug in your lamp. The other one goes over the area you want to light up. Hang your light on these hooks. Secure the cord to the hooks with twist ties.

SECRET TREASURE BOOK BOX

Do you need a place to keep something special? Make a box out of an old book. Put it on your shelf with other books. No one will know it hides treasures! You will be using a box cutter. Ask an adult to help.

MATERIALS

- A thick book with a hard cover (make sure it is an old book that no one wants to read anymore!)
- Ruler
- Pencil
- Box cutter
- Large binder clip
- Water-based varnish
- Sponge brush
- Paper plate palette

STEPS

1. Open your book. Measure a frame. It needs at least a 1-inch (2.5 cm) border. Mark it on the first page.

2. Hold the ruler along the lines of the frame. Use the box cutter to cut around the frame. Cut as deep as you can through the pages. Remove the paper from inside the frame.

3. Clip the cut pages to the book's front cover. This keeps them out of the way. Use one of the cut pages as a guide. Cut through the next bunch of pages. Use a ruler to keep the lines straight. Keep all of the pages lined up.

4. Repeat step 3 until you have cut through most of the pages. Leave about a 0.5-inch (1.3 cm) of pages at the end of the book.

SEE NEXT PAGE ➡

5. Next you will glue down all the pages. Start from the back of the book. Use a paper plate as a palette to hold the varnish. Dip your sponge brush in the varnish. Spread it on the inside of the back cover. Press down the last page onto the back cover.

6. For every 0.25 inch (0.6 cm) of pages, paint a page with varnish. Cover the entire surface. Press down the pages after it. Continue until you reach the framed pages.

7. Spread varnish all around the frame. Press down the pages in sections. Like in step 6. Do not spread varnish on the first page. (The front cover needs to open like a lid.)

8. Close the book. Make sure all of the pages are lined up. Like a block. Paint around the three sides of the block of pages. Use a lot of varnish. Make sure the top cover can still open. Wipe off any varnish that may make it stick. Then close the book tightly. Seal it with rubber bands. Let it sit for an hour. The varnish will dry and harden.

9. Open the cover. Spread varnish all around the frame of the first page. Spread it on the sides and bottom of the hole. Spread a second coat of varnish around the sides of the book block. Leave the front cover open. Let the varnish dry.

DO YOUR PART—
TOGETHER!

Host a recycling party! Make invitations. Use scraps of paper from magazines or wrapping paper. Invite your friends over to make crafts. Ask them to bring materials to reuse. Share ideas and supplies. Let your imaginations fly!

You are helping Earth when you recycle. You are reducing the amount of trash in landfills. When you turn those things into beautiful crafts, you are doing something else important for Earth, too. You are making it a little more beautiful with your art!

GLOSSARY

adhesives (ad-HEE-sivz) substances, such as glue, that make things stick together

decompose (dee-kuhm-POZE) to break down into soil

diameter (dye-AA-muh-tuhr) a straight line through the center of a circle, connecting opposite sides

flexible (FLEK-suh-buhl) able to bend

hems (HEMZ) edges of material that have been folded over and sewn down

palette (PAH-luht) a flat surface that is used for mixing paints

pulp (PUHLP) any soft, wet mixture

recycling (ree-SYE-kling) preparing old items, such as glass, plastic, newspapers, and aluminum cans, to be made into new products

FOR MORE INFORMATION

BOOKS

Enz, Tammy. *Repurpose It: Invent New Uses for Old Stuff*. Mankato, MN: Capstone Press, 2012.

Friday, Megan. *Green Crafts: Become an Earth-Friendly Craft Star, Step by Easy Step!* Irvine, CA: Walter Foster Pub., 2011.

Gardner, Robert. *Recycle: Green Science Projects for a Sustainable Planet*. Berkeley Heights, NJ: Enslow Publishers, 2011.

Rau, Dana Meachen. *Plastic*. New York: Marshall Cavendish Benchmark, 2012.

Scheunemann, Pam. Cool *Odds and Ends Projects: Creative Ways to Upcycle Your Trash into Treasure*. Minneapolis: ABDO Publishing Company, 2013.

INDEX